Kittens

●ANIMAL BABIES SERIES●

Kittens

English language version © Copyright
Barron's Educational Series, Inc., 2000

Original title of the book in Spanish:
Ciencias y Manualidades de Animales Bebe

© Copyright Useful Books S.L., 1999
Barcelona, Spain (World Rights)

All inquiries should be addressed to:
Barron's Educational Series, Inc.
250 Wireless Boulevard
Hauppauge, New York 11788
http://www.barronseduc.com

Author of the scientific text: Norbert Landa
Author of the crafts text: Ona Pons
Crafts execution: Victoria Seix

Series graphic design: Estudi Guasch

Photography: Index and Age Fotostock
                    Nos & Soto

ISBN: 0-7641-1481-6

Library of Congress Catalog Card No. 99-068583

Printed in Spain
9 8 7 6 5 4 3 2

Kittens

Facts:

Fun:

Do you like kittens?

Of course you do! Kittens are cute and they are fun to play with, although remember they are animals and not toys. They need you to love them and take care of them.

How do kittens talk?

Kittens talk to one another by meowing in different ways, but you can also learn to understand what they say. What is your kitten saying now? "Look, I'm here!," or "I feel lonely!," or "I'm hungry!"

When cats feel happy, they purr. This is something baby kittens have to learn how to do.

Are all cats the same?

There are house cats that live at home with us, wild cats that live in the woods, and big cats like lions, tigers, and leopards that live in jungles or mountains. The kittens of all these cats all look alike when they are first born.

But when they grow up, tigers, panthers, and lions become big, wild, and dangerous animals. Domestic cats, however, stay fairly small and enjoy being with people. They will not attack unless they feel threatened.

Why do kittens have sharp claws?

Kittens like to keep their claws sharp so they can climb trees and hunt mice. Surprise! Where are the claws now? They are hidden because the kitten doesn't need them. His paws are so soft now that they don't make any noise when he walks.

How does the mother cat take care of her kittens?

Mother cat feeds her kittens with her milk, just like other mothers do. Human babies, puppies, and calves also drink their mother's milk.

Mother cat keeps her kittens out of harm's way, and teaches them how to wash themselves. Cats are very clean animals.

Kittens

What do kittens have to learn?

Kittens have to learn how to behave like cats—that's why they imitate what their mothers do: Climbing trees or jumping to high places, hiding, and looking for the nicest, safest place to sleep.

When kittens are playing, they are also learning how to attack, surprise, chase, explore, and defend themselves. They will need to do all these things when they become adults.

What do kittens like to eat?

Kittens only need to drink their mother's milk, and very young kittens need plenty of it. The milk from any other animals, like a cow, can make them sick.

When they are a few weeks old, they start eating solid food. What they like best is a mix of meat, vegetables, and cereals like the cat food you can buy at the store.

Where do kittens live ?

The best home for a domestic cat is a house with a yard or an apartment on the ground floor, so he can go in and out as he likes.

Cats can sleep for hours during the day, but they like to go out for a walk or hunting at night. Have you ever seen how their eyes shine? They can see very well in the dark.

You will need the following materials:

Tissue paper (white, orange, red, black, and blue); bristol board, a stick of glue, a pencil, scissors, and a photograph.

A colorful kitten to hold a picture of your favorite friend.

A tricolored pussycat

1 Place the photo on the bristol board and trace its outline using a pencil.

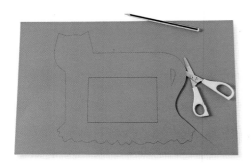

2 Now draw the outline of the cat. Leave a margin at the bottom and draw an irregular outline to represent grass. Cut out the figure.

3 Cut out a window that is smaller than the picture right where the picture should be. Cut the window in half so you can open and close it.

4 Tear a bunch of small pieces of tissue paper and roll them into tiny balls. Use some glue to stick them all over the pussycat.

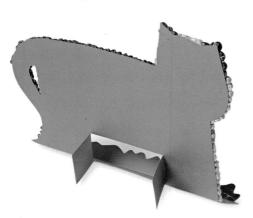

5 Roll strips of black tissue paper for the whiskers. A triangle will do for a nose and for eyes you can make two bigger balls with blue tissue paper. Use some glue to stick everything onto the cat.

6 Fold back the window and glue the picture into place.

7 Fold the base forward, leave the margin flat and fold it again so the grass will stand up.

Kittens

You will need the following materials:

Brown bristol board,
a black marker, a pencil, scissors,
and a stick of glue.

Your kitten sleeps while you enjoy a story.

A sleepy bookmark

1 Following the template on page 31, draw the sleeping cat figure twice, once on each side, on the brown bristol board.

2 Cut out both figures of the sleeping cat.

3 Use the black marker to draw the edge of both figures.

4 Apply some glue to the back of the upper part of one of the figures, place the other figure on top, and press to glue.

5 When dry, you can separate both parts a little at the bottom and insert a page from your favorite storybook.

Catching a fish is difficult!

The gray and black kitten

You will need the following materials:

Plastic (transparent and gray), adhesive plastic (yellow, orange, and black), two markers (blue and black), a white sticker, sewing thread, a ribbon, two bookbinding clips, a hole puncher, scissors, a pencil, white glue, a small brush, and a disposable container.

1 Trace the template on page 31. Draw the fish tank on the transparent plastic and the kitten and the paw on the gray plastic. Mark the holes.

2 Cut out the outline of the fish tank, the kitten and its paw, and punch out the marked holes.

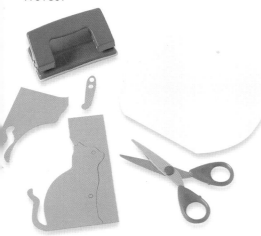

3 Use the blue marker to color all but the upper part of the fish tank. Put some white glue in a disposable container and apply the glue with a brush all over the marker. Let dry.

4 Draw spots for the cat on the black adhesive plastic and cut them out. Mark and punch the holes. Glue everything and draw the face with a marker. Cut out a yellow fish and an orange fish from the corresponding adhesive plastics.

5 Tie some thread to the first hole in the paw. Align the other hole in the paw with the hole in the cat and put a bookbinding clip through. Open its flaps, but not too tightly.

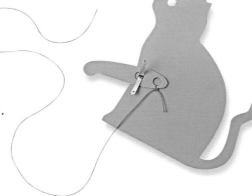

7 Glue the fish in place and tie a ribbon to the upper hole in the fish tank. If you pull the thread lightly, maybe your kitten will catch a fish!

6 Place the cat over the fish tank, mark the eye and punch it together with the fish tank. Put a bookbinding clip through, fold back its flaps, and place a white sticker with a black line where the eye goes.

You will need the following materials:

Cloth (yellow, orange, white, and black), Velcro, a pencil, scissors, and white glue.

Mother cat looks after and trains her kittens.

A cat family pajama bag

1 Fold the yellow cloth in half. Use the template on page 30 to draw the outside figure, the decoration with the kittens, and the head of one of them on the cloth. Cut out the outline of the figures.

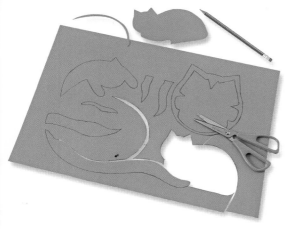

3 Cut out the details for the faces from the black cloth and eyes from the white cloth.

2 On the orange cloth, draw and cut out the two kittens and the decorations for the mother cat.

4 Apply white glue all around the edge of each yellow piece but *not* at the bottom part. Place the other piece on top and press them together.

5 Use some white glue to stick the decorations in place. Let dry.

6 Glue the Velcro to the inside of the bottom part of the bag. Now you can keep your pajamas in it!

Kittens

27

You like candy, he likes milk.

A Siamese cat at a party

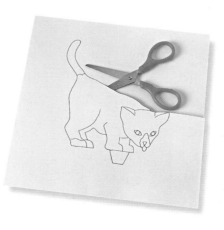

1 Use the template on page 31 to draw the figure of the Siamese cat on the beige bristol board. Cut out the outline.

2 Use the markers to paint the details.

3 Make a wide strip of blue corrugated cardboard, fold a margin and cut triangles out of it. Make a ring with the strip and glue both ends together.

4 Place the cylinder over the blue corrugated paper and mark the inside circle with a pencil. Draw the bigger circle. Cut out the outline of both circles and use the bigger one to make another just like it.

5 Apply some glue to the whole circle, except where the cup goes. Place the cup in the open circle and glue together the two big circles.

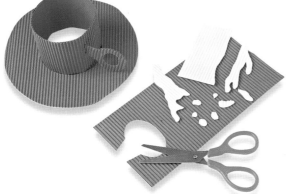

6 Draw the handle and cut out its outline. Make a vertical slit in the cup so the flap can go through. Cut out the milk splotches from the white corrugated cardboard.

7 Glue the handle and the white splotches to the cup. Fold the flap in the cat under the cup. Now it is ready to be filled with all kinds of candy for your party.

Templates

Place some tracing paper over the template you want to copy. Trace the outline with a pencil. Turn the tracing paper over and retrace the outline over the chosen bristol or cardboard.

A cat family pajama bag, page 26

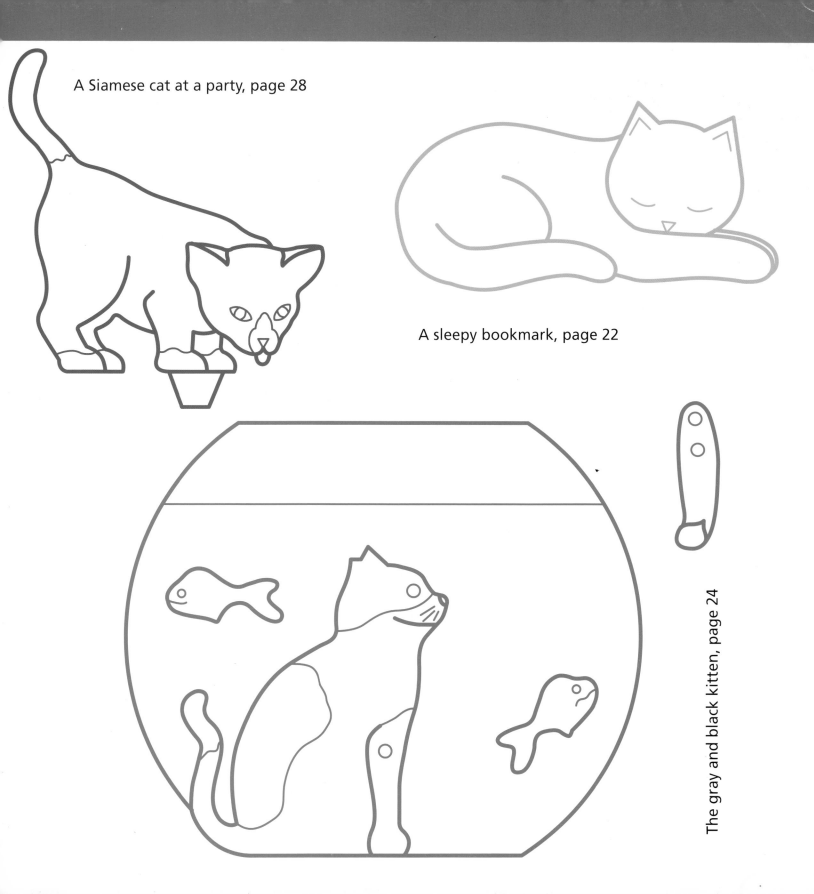

A Siamese cat at a party, page 28

A sleepy bookmark, page 22

The gray and black kitten, page 24

Kittens

When Kitten comes home from a walk
She and I begin to talk
She walks up to me and says "meow"
And lets me know she's here now.

Kitten says "meow"
and Kitten says "purr"
I love how she says it
because I love her.

Kitten comes home with the first
morning light
And now I learn where she has been
And what kind of things she has done
through the night
and which kind of things she has seen.

The story goes "meow"
And the story goes "purr"
I am terribly sorry
I cannot translate the story
It's a secret between me and her.

Kitten and I